IF ONLY I COULD TELL YOU

IF ONLY

Poems for Young Lovers

I COULD

and Dreamers

TELL YOU

by Eve Merriam

With illustrations by Donna Diamond

Alfred A. Knopf ✦ *New York*

THIS IS A BORZOI BOOK PUBLISHED BY ALFRED A. KNOPF, INC.
Text Copyright © 1983 by Eve Merriam
Illustrations Copyright © 1983 by Donna Diamond
All rights reserved under International and Pan-American
Copyright Conventions. Published in the United States
by Alfred A. Knopf, Inc., New York, and simultaneously
in Canada by Random House of Canada Limited, Toronto.
Distributed by Random House, Inc., New York.
Designed by Mimi Harrison
10 9 8 7 6 5 4 3 2 1
Manufactured in the United States of America

Library of Congress Cataloging in Publication Data
Merriam, Eve, 1916–If only I could tell you.
Summary: A collection of more than fifty poems
emphasizing love and other emotions.
[1. Love–Poetry. 2. American poetry]
I. Diamond, Donna, ill, II. Title.
PS3525.E639I33 1983   811'.54   83-4377
ISBN 0-394-86043-8   ISBN 0-394-96043-2 (lib. bdg.)

For the past and the future

with Waldo

CONTENTS

IF ONLY I COULD TELL YOU

GOOD MORNING

A mirror reflects us together:
love in a jacket,
love in a T-shirt,
love wearing sneakers.

You smile at me
and kisses curl in the air like autumn leaves,
the newspaper under my arm refuses all words of war.
All that we read is the weather report:
forecast of stars, flowers, fair and forever.

Good morning.

NIGHT SCENE

I make no magic claims
only
I have so arranged things
that you can never look
at the new moon
or the full moon
without thinking of me

SIZING UP

I want to be smaller
than a computer chip
so that wherever you go
I can slip in

to a corner of your wallet
the lining of your glove
even burrow under the buttons of your vest.

THE PRESENCE OF ABSENCE

When you're away
I'm a single shoe

pockets without a coat

a hat

and no head to put it on

PROGRAMMING

*H*ow would we be on Teevee?

No sitcom
with canned laughter on a track;
we cry natural tears.

No game show
with giveaways and jumping jackpots;
we're each other's prize.

And we couldn't be guests of the
late night comedy hour because
it's no joke even though we laugh
at the miracle of meeting.

I think a simple newsbreak:
now here's the big story folks hot off the wire—
This Twosome Getting Together!

UNTITLED

I speak wordlessly to you

Will you answer me?

In the silence

I hear you.

A CHANGE IN THE WEATHER

The day got off to a rotten start
the alarm didn't ring
I broke a shoelace
burnt the toast
slammed the door with my keys inside

there was ice on the sidewalk I
didn't see the curb
almost sprained my ankle
spilled my lunch bag
broke the zipper on my jacket

it was going to be one of those days
jinxed
hexed
hapless
hopeless

so hang in and hold on for tomorrow
when like a genie out of a bottle
a magic presence appeared
loping along with your gait
wearing your sweater and scarf
and boots and wink and grin.

SECRET PAGES

I want to be a notebook
that can fit into your pocket

the pages turning to reveal
secret poems

the poems
invisible and necessary as air
surrounding you

simile poems
all the delights of the world
that I can liken unto you

and one metaphor poem
as we become each other

SUMMER VACATION

After Christina Rosetti

What is fragrant?
The meadow in clover.

What is golden?
The sunset on water.

What is endless?
The long days of summer.

What is sorrow?
The summer is over.

YOUR HAIR

Your hair
is a web
of Japanese silk
for me to
weave my fingers through

15

*L*ike bookends
   my father at one side
   my mother at the other

   propping me up
   but unable to read
   what I feel.

Were they born with clothes on?
Born with rules on?

When we sit at the dinner table
we smooth our napkins into polite folds.
How was your day dear
                Fine
And how was yours dear
                Fine
And how was school
              The same

Only once in a while
when we're not trying so hard
when we're not trying at all
our napkins suddenly whirl away
and we float up to the ceiling
where we sing and dance until it hurts from laughing

and then we float down
with our napkin parachutes
and once again spoon our soup
and pass the bread please.

MY ACROBATIC CIRCUS DREAM

to crash through

the hoop of

separation

and

land

softly

in your arms

ENTERING MY LIFE

That day
oh that day
there should have been
a wild sign

a rush of
white doves
like snowflakes
falling upward

rivers
turning purple as berries
traffic lights
melting into parks

a wild sign
to let me know
that was the day
I would see you for the first time

ARISING

$\mathcal{E}$very morning
when I awaken
I open the cage of my mouth
and your name
flies forth.

SOLITAIRE

When you are gone
I feel as flat and dull
as plastic cards

shuffle and reshuffle
the surface slick easy to wipe off
the edges rounded harmless

then you appear
and I fling the cards
like fireworks

they fall into
a winning pattern
look a perfect run of hearts

7 8 9 10 J Q

ARITHMETIC LESSON

One and one
are two
of course

but sometimes
when our steps
precisely match

you can see
that two
are one

then times
when we're apart
you can take

one
from two and
nothing's left

SYMBIOTIC

You're the moonlight
I'm the dark

You're the ocean
I'm the fish

You're the tower
I'm the stone

You're the wishbone
make me
your wish

MY IMAGINARY RAINY DAY POEM

*I*t is raining out
so I take my umbrella
and when I put it up

the rain turns into
rose petals
and my umbrella

rises
to become
an airship

where you
are the pilot
and I am the only passenger

FIRST STAR

*C*oming home after school
  on this late winter afternoon
  my fingers are tingling
    inside my woolen gloves
  I have to keep wriggling my toes
    inside my heavy boots
  my breath is visible in the air
    like tiny jet plane trails
  and I'm hugging my books to keep warm

  the sky is already dark
  I can see the first star
  I'm making a wish
  that on Saturday night
  when I get up to dance
  no one will clap
  and no one will groan

they'll all just take me for granted
as though I've always been
part of the crowd

THREE WAYS TO FLY

*W*ings on a skylark
fins on a dolphin
your hands touching me

EXPRESSION

*M*y aunt says
when she was my age
they used to talk about
getting a crush on someone.

It's an expression that's out of fashion.
No wonder.
I wouldn't want to
have a crush on anybody:
that way,
you'd be leaning on the person hard,
so closed in
they could get to feel almost strangled
and you could feel
that you'd never be able
to stand up
for yourself.

T.V.

No one else in the world
has a television set like mine

it is unique
custom-made to my specifications

handily portable
yet with a grandiose screen

an infinite number of channels
all finely tuned

the mix of sound and picture
perfectly in balance

the color
amazingly lifelike and true

the programs
changing at my whim

always new and varied
with but one constant:

the central character in every show
continues to be you

THE ROOT

*J*ealousy
why can't I let it go?

jealousy jealousy
why is it as though

I have to keep on watering
a twisted root

that can only grow
into a twisted tree

don't I know
that tree can only bear

one fruit
the sour fruit

of jealousy?

VIEWPOINT

Sometimes when the tide
is on the way in
it looks as if
it is on the way out.

I remind myself of that
when I think about
our fight
last night.

DIRECTIONS FOR DRIVING

*I*f you were
next to me
in the car

I would drive
to the top of
Lookout Mountain

and change
the sign there
so that it would read:

"Don't bother with
the advertised
fabulous view,

get back in the car
and gaze
alongside."

MULTIPLE CHOICE

Underline the correct answer:

a

b

c

?

You are my entire alphabet.

I.D.

When they ask for identification
I know they expect me
to take out my wallet
and flash that plastic card

with a bunch of numbers on it
and my name
and my address
and the worst picture I've ever taken in my life.

How can I show them
my true I. D.?
I'm no longer the person
I was before I met you.

MISTER TOMORROW

*M*ister Tomorrow,
what will you bring?
Velveteen snowflakes,
harlequin rain?
Feathers of sorrow,
pillows of pain?

Mister Tomorrow,
what will you wear?
Porcupine pants or
dollar-bill suits?
Prisoner's jacket,
liberty boots?

Mister Tomorrow,
I'm longing to see.
Are you coming tonight?
Are you coming today?
Are you coming to me?

IN MY BACKPACK

*E*verything I need for the exam:
books
     ballpoint
          spiral notepad

and with it all
my good luck charm
that reminds me of you

I have it stowed away
at the bottom of the pack
so I won't even see it

then luckily
I'll be able to concentrate
strictly on the exam.

THE LINE

When there's silence on your end,
the telephone line
is a strangling rope,
a dark jungle vine;

but let your voice
respond to mine:
then the knots untangle
and everything's fine.

CONGRATULATIONS

*F*or your birthday
a piece
of cake:

stars sprinkled on top of
a slice of the moon
heaped on a plate of the sun:

for you alone
only you'll insist
on sharing it with me.

MAYBE

$\mathcal{T}$omorrow
may be the day
that you won't look
through me.

Instead
you'll stop
and look
into me.

GRAFFITI

*H*ow can we link ourselves
for the world to see?

Whittle initials
in a heart on a tree?

Buy matching T-shirts
labeled YOU and ME?

Photocopy our faces
innumerably?

What type of graffiti
will survive?

> *The snapshots of memory*
> *stay most alive.*

TWO PEOPLE I WANT TO BE LIKE

That man
stuck in traffic
not pounding his fists against the steering wheel
not trying to shift to the next lane
just
using the time
for a slow steady grin
of remembering
all the good unstuck times

and that woman
clerking in the supermarket
at rush hour
bagging bottles and cartons and boxes and
jars and cans

punching it all out
slapping it all along
and leveling a smile
at everyone in the line.

I wish they were married to each other.

Maybe it's better they're not,
so they can pass their sweet harmony around.

NINE RULES I'D LIKE TO POST
FOR MY PARENTS

1. Don't listen in on the telephone.

2. Don't ask, "How can you wear *that?*"

3. Don't turn down the music before you turn it up.

4. Don't raise the topic of sex
   unless you're willing to take the time
   for a long leisurely unself-conscious chat.

5. Don't volunteer me as a baby-sitter.

6. Don't suggest a parakeet instead of a dog or a cat.

7. Don't read my mail—not even postcards.

8. Don't laugh when I don't want to be laughed at.

9. Don't tell me how much things cost
when you were in your teens.

CAREFUL

*H*ow tenderly
I can unfold
the word for *you*
into
the intimacy
of *thee*
and *thou*

however
us
I cannot touch,
the paint is still too fresh.

TO THE PERSON ADDRESSED AS *YOU* IN MY SECRET DIARY

I don't have to spell out your name,
you know who you are.

GAME PLAY

I'm inventing a new video game
it's modeled on a telephone switchboard

the instructions are simple to follow
all you need to know is that

it's for two players at a time
and whoever makes the opening move

the board lights up
and flashes

CALL ME
CALL ME
CALL ME
CALL ME

CALL ME
CALL ME
CALL ME

soon?

please?

AS USUAL

One day I'll be opening the mailbox
and the usual will be there:
a catalogue for camping gear,
a ten-cents-off coupon for cheese spread,
a Dear Occupant card.

I'll take out all the junk mail
and put my hand back into the empty box
and there will be
a feather
or
a petal
or
a fern
and I'll recognize your signature.

There was once a group named
The Lovin' Spoonful

Why set limits?

Why not
Bowlfuls
Tablefuls
Truckfuls
Land Sky and Seafuls?

YOU'RE GONE

How do I feel,
people ask.

How do I feel?
That's the problem.

I don't.

THINKING OF YOU

*A*t night

in the dark

thinking of you

the sky

becomes

so bright

I have to

put on

sunglasses.

QUESTION MARKS

*W*hat does it mean to
"go together"?

Do you both order club sandwiches,
get two straws for one soda?

Do you finish each other's sentences?

Are you always in
each other's company,
with no time off for good behavior?

Are your ideas permanently joined,
are your eyes level,
gazing at the same horizon?

Are you never alone,
do you share everything—
even dreams and nightmares?

Are you stuck there?
Might there be times you'd like to come apart?

ON HER FEET

*M*y best friend wears sneakers
even when it snows.

She says they're like snow,
soft and soundless,
they make her feel invisible,
times when she needs to be.

She says when she wears heels
they click with authority,
they keep making important sounds
as if she should be thinking of
something to say that's really significant.

With sneakers she can curve around corners
instead of having to bump straight on
into the right angles.

EPISODE

You came with someone else
and now you want to leave with me

it's confusing like entering a theater
when the movie's already under way

I don't know the characters yet
I don't know where the action's heading

I think I'd better wait
for the next showing.

EQUALS

*W*ho bakes the cake?
Who takes the check?

Good-bye to the dumb old days
of raising boys in blue
and girls in pink.

Out on a date
there's cool equality.
Divide by two.
Or flip a coin to see who pays.

But whose coin
from whose wallet?

And who goes first?

Sometimes
out of the dumb old past
shadows still are cast.

THIS GIRL AND THIS BOY

*L*ook at them laughing,
their arms around each other
like Christmas wrappings.

The world is theirs:
they can loop it in a bow or knot it
and cut it off with fringes;

they're on the verge of dancing,
a secret little dance they teach each other

while they're looking straight at the camera,
daring it to capture their bliss—

in a moment they'll stick out their tongues,
forgetting they're very nearly grownups now—

I wish I knew them,
this larky girl and boy I've never met.

I study the old photograph
of my mother and my father.

IT'S GRAND

Why is it easier
with a grand
than with a parent?

You can lean your heads together
and tell stupid monster jokes
and sneak candy
and watch too much television
and whisper behind your hands
about how foolishly stern
your mother is.

Oh mydearyes, grandma puts on her best frown,
she's as bad as my own daughter,
and you both crack up.

MORNING SOUNDS

 he pollution begins:

oil trucks choking
blast of bulldozers
white-hot whine of police and ambulance sirens
brazen clang of fire engines
the smoke coughing and clatter of everyday life

and above it all
one clear flute note:
it is dawn
and I share my presence in this world with you.

The North Star

A blaze on a tree in the woods

The light of your voice

LIBRARY LOVE

A hand reaches for the book next to mine
an accidental touch
we blush

you can hear the quiet
as we take seats facing each other
pretending it's not on purpose

our feelings on tiptoe
our blushes louder
Shh!

turn pages in nervous anticipation
the paper rustles like bonfire
how can we tamp it down?

so much to exchange with one another
but we can't talk here
nodding we rise as one

outside on the steps
in the sunlight of everyday
away from romantic silence

what is there to say?

PORTENT

*I*t was fated for us to meet:
there was a double rainbow in the sky that day.

Now you've moved away.
Why?
Can there be a double rainbow in another sky?

SELF-IMAGE

*S*ometimes when I'm waiting
for the traffic light to change
I smile and close my eyes

and see you held captive
in a castle on a rocky cliff
where I'm climbing to your rescue

or else we're rocketing to the planet Zore
where every winged creature
and all the trees and flowers are gleaming silver:

then the light changes
and I open my eyes
and cross the street.

Who is that extraordinary person
with the mysterious smile
I hope everyone is thinking.

*H*ow does it *really* feel?

It's hard to say
it's like trying to talk when you're swimming
you don't

you just float in the lake
with the sun warming the water

you could bask there forever
it's the same temperature as your skin

you hardly feel any difference at all
you feel so at home

Eve Merriam has won many awards for
her poetry, from the Yale Younger Poets
Award at the beginning of her career to
the 1981 NCTE Excellence in Poetry for
Children Award. The author of over
forty books for adults and children, Ms.
Merriam is also a playwright with an
Obie to her credit. Her articles and
poems appear often in national
magazines. She is the mother of two sons
and lives in New York City.

If Only I Could Tell You grew out of Ms.
Merriam's readings across the country,
where she was frequently asked by young
people to write a book of love poems
especially for them.